MACOS BIG SUR FOR BEGINNERS

A PRACTICAL GUIDE FOR GETTING
STARTED ON
MACOS BIG SUR WITH TIPS AND TRICKS

EILEEN D. ROSENBERG

i

Copyright

Contents

CHAPTER ONE

WHAT THE TERM MACOS BIG SUR IS ALL ABOUT

Definition of macOS

macOS is an operating system that controls the whole Mac computers just like there's Windows on Personal Computers. Different from Windows, macOS is merely supplied with Apple Computers. A lot of users say that the system operation is among their motive for getting Apple hardware. Usually, the system operation gets frequent updates on security and the main upgrade every year. Before now, macOS was known as Mac OS X, wherein the first version was called (10.0) debuted in 2001.

Therefore, macOS is a properly direct operating system that comes with a great collection of apps to make the everyday task easier like web browsing and email.

Apple and an operating system design it. This system operation is what enables you to make use of a computer. It comes as preloaded on every new Apple Macintosh computers (usually called Macs) making it possible for you to complete all form of different tasks on your Personal Computer.

For instance, it can be used to surfing the web, playing games, listening to music, checking an email, editing digital photos. macOS is used in various offices due to its ability to dispose of tools like Word Processors, Spreadsheets and Calendars for productivity access.

Previous macOS versions are within the mid-1980s. However, there had been a lot of versions since then. Nevertheless, the most current ones are macOS Mojave (2018), High Sierra (2017), Sierra (2016). El Capitan (2015), and Yosemite (2014).

Some previous version calls it OS X (pronounced O-S ten), therefore, a lot of persons now use the term macOS and OS X alternatively since the fundamental functions of the operating system is still very much similar.

Definition macOS Big Sur

macOS Big Sur is defined as an extension of Apple functioning system powering its mobile and desktop computers as they are lined up. It's carrying the name 'macOS' because it is the first main version adjusted in 15years and dropping the 10.x and going by 11.x officially.

macOS Big Sur carries with it a lot of firsts for Apple's latest operating system. Thereby continue to expand more on some of the adjustments made in preceding versions to unite the experience of the desktop with the greatest of its mobile OS--iOS/iPadOS—creating a user-friendly computing environment that is unparalleled and powerful in its ease.

Different from preceding versions of the macOS, Big Sur that doesn't have any minimum set of basic requirements on hardware components. Rather, Apple has brought the least type of hardware-based on its desktop computers and mobile lined up and the year it was released to serve as a useful guide.

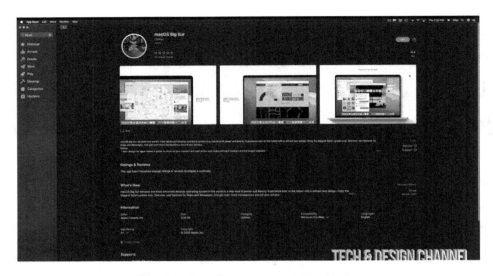

A screen displaying how macOS Big Sur appears

THE MAIN FEATURES OF MACOS BIG SUR

Control Center for Mac

Similar to its iPadOS /iOS counterpart, Mac Control Center made a move with macOS Big Sur, given that one-click can have access to various functions to control several features and connections that are common, such as Bluetooth and Wi-Fi, modifying your screen settings to suit your current work environment or playing music. Other controls can be included to modify the experience-based according to your preference.

App integration

It was announced by Apple as at November 2020 during its event that all Apple's Mac apps are currently running natively for M1 system and universal. Mac applications that are already existing and haven't been upgraded to General will now run with Apple's Rosetta 2 technology with translations application for a system that runs intel chips. That is, applications on the iPad and iPhone can now directly run on the Mac.

Notification Center

Although notifications were first introduced in previous versions, macOS Big Sur's restructured in a way that it enables notifications to be grouped by applications for management at ease.

Also, notifications and widgets are now shown together inside similar window to enable unity in its look and relevant information at a glimpse.

Safari 14

This has had main efficiency, visual. Privacy fixing to upsurge usability to enable the in-built customizations for an individual user, the battery life amendments for more productivity, and preserve tabs of various sites and internet applications that are also doing their best to keep tabs on you and your data by notifying you if the password used for the site have been jeopardized. Safari now offers 'Privacy Report' every week on 'Intelligent Tracking Prevention' so you can see the protection of your privacy as a result of the sites that was visited while bringing a snapshot of the way trackers through the web are summarizing users.

Safari is presently 1.5 times quicker to run JavaScript and almost two times more reactive.

Messages

There's no advantage and capacity to pin vital conversations to appear above your list of chat for rapid response and assessment. Conversations that are pinned are sync through the Apple's ecosystem with iPadOS 14/iOS devices enabled and macOS Big Sur supporting device. An additional feature of usability is 'inline replies' that enable users to directly respond to a particular message, thereby tagging the message as thread, enabling track keeping of replies pretty much easier.

Guides and Maps

Maps are redesigned, enabling the navigation application to take total advantage of bigger screen afforded by a higher resolution founded on a new Macs and 4K/5K monitors. A new direction for an electrical form of vehicles has been added enabling users to propose a better direction to add charging stops alongside the way. Talking about stops, Guides gives a curated endpoint of the better places where you can visit or your best spots. It may be made by you or for you and commonly shared for stress-free access.

Application Store privacy

The major success for advocating privacy and a large step towards transparency is privacy data summary added for every application in your Mac App Store. Related to labels discovered on other consumers product purchase, such private summary will add information on the types of information developers gather, the way they will gather it, as well as what they will do with such data as well as if will be used in movement tracking through the internet.

New language features

Various bilingual dictionaries have been introduced on the macOS Big Sur for ease of translation among different languages, like German to French, English to Polish, Chinese to Japanese. Also, improved predictive feature for Japanese and Chinese had been added for better accuracy and relative predictions. Additional fonts are now included with upgrades to the existing ones for India as well as localized massage effects.

Apple Silicon support

Earlier on, Apple publicized its plans of switching from Intel CPUs to the processor of its design built on ARM architecture at WWDC 20.

Apple, Apple M1 has replaced the current Intel-based elements with its SOC. Whereby; the transition is expected to last for two years, in due course subsequent in all its devices organizing its branded SoC, beginning with the first products, such as the MacBook Air with M1, MacBook Pro with M1, and Mac mini with M1.

System Security

In line with the efforts to continuously harden macOS while protecting user's information, Big Sur enlarge on its system volume improvements made by the graphical crypto signing of the volume, that ensure when macOS 11.0 is installed, the system volume produces a key certifying the reliability of the volume.

Devices supporting macOS Big Sur

Thoroughly, Apple examines the functioning system a newly released device to ensure compatibility within existing devices. The technique for testing and authentication remains with macOS Big Sur, as well as the list generated officially by Apple included below.

- MacBook (2015 and newer)
- MacBook Air (2013 and newer)
- MacBook Air with M1
- MacBook Pro (Late-2013 and newer)
- MacBook Pro with M1
- iMac (2014 and newer)
- iMac Pro (2017 and newer)
- Mac Pro (2013 and newer)

- Mac mini (2014 and newer)
- Mac mini with M1

CHAPTER TWO

INSTALLING MACOS BIG SUR

Here's how to install macOS Big Sur on your Mac, as well as a workaround since some persons are finding it difficult in downloading and installing it.

The macOS Big Sur 11 originates with a main visual examination influenced by iOS, has an original Control Center, widgets, lots of Safari improvements, new Notifications Center, and so on. Nevertheless, it's certainly better to ruminate if it's best to upgrade before you make a jump.

How to install macOS Big Sur on your Mac

macOS 11.0.1 happens to be an innovative public release weighs up to 12GB in size. You'll therefore require about 16GB of free disk space to download it and bear in mind that it may take some hours or more to download completely; it also depends on your internet connection and Apple's servers.

You can begin your download, or you can search the Mac App Store for 'Big Sur'

- Tap the "Blue Get" button
- On the System Preferences window that would pop up, tap "Download."
- Upon the completion of the download (note that it may take some hours) the installer will open automatically (supposing an error pops up, you can try again)
- Tap "Continue", then follow the directives
- Please during the installation process ensure you do not close the lid of your MacBook or put your Mac to sleep.

Downloading and installing macOS updates

- Tap on the "Apple icon" at the left upper corner of the screen
- Click "System preferences" from your drop-down menu
- Tap "Software Update"
- Tap "Update Now" close to macOS update.
- Click "Continue"
- Read the Terms and Condition and tap "Agree"
- Tap "Continue"

- Enter "Password" and click "Ok" while you wait for installation
- Click "Restart" icon
- The Mac will have to restart once the download has been successfully installed; therefore, ensure that your progress is saved in any program you're working on currently.

Note: The restarting may take some time. Therefore, be patient.

Turning on your automatic updates

Your macOS doesn't have to be manually updated each time a new one is launched. Turn on the automatic updates, and it will be downloaded in the background.

- Tap on the "Apple icon" at the left upper corner of the screen
- Click "System preferences" from your drop-down menu
- Tap "Software Update"
- Check the box to keep your Mac Automatically up to date.

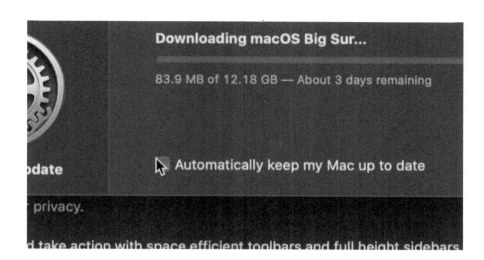

CHAPTER THREE

CUSTOMIZING ON MACOS BIG SUR

macOS Big Sur is a current operating system, and it is the highest overhaul that Apple's desktop OS has had in years. Together with a whole new contemporary visual reforming, it brings an entire host for customizing options making it easier to place your stamp on the Mac. How exciting!

Even if the feature is new such as Tweaks or Control Center to recent application and workflows, macOS Big Sur has sufficient tools to enable you to shape it according to how you like it.

This book will reveal some better ways of customizing your Mac and how you can use them.

Customizing Control Center

A biggest new additions to macOS Big Sur is the Control Center.

Just like in the iOS 14, this your one-stop shop for easy options and controls to tweak macOS settings on the go. To have access to it:

- Tap "Control Center" icon that appears like two toggles at the top right of the screen

Note: The settings that displays in Control Center can be adjusted when you:

- Open "System Preferences"
- Tap "Dock & Menu" bar
- At the left-hand toolbar, also, discover the heading of the Control Center.
- Tap an option below it to select if it should display in your Control Center, menu bar or even both.

Include settings to your menu bar

Customization potentials accessible through Control Center is not only restricted to Control Center. In short, switches and settings can be dragged out onto a menu bar, while storing them in a location to easily access it without going to open the Control Center ever.

To achieve this:

- Tap "Control Center" icon,
- Tap and drag a particular setting on the menu bar.
- Then the current icon of your menu bar will move automatically to avoid obstruction.

Note: This works fine with settings that are commonly used such as Bluetooth and AirDrop, particularly when you discovered you're toggling them quite a lot of times per day. And that, including the sound and brightness settings can frequently help you reaching for the function keys or Touch Bar.

Widgets in Notification Centers

Control Center does not only have the feature sharing links with iOS 14, such as in the Apple's mobile functioning system, but macOS Big Sur also enable you to include widgets to ease your workflow. Though it cannot be included to the desktop, rather dwell in the refitted Notification Center. For you to access it:

- Tap the date and time at the top right corner
- Scroll to underneath the list
- Tap "Edit Widgets"
- A screen would display having three columns with widgets and applications to select from at the left-hand side, you've presently selected widget at the middle (majorly with various options of size) with widgets at your right already at Notification Center.

You can easily drag and drop widgets on the Notification Center while rearranging recent ones with just a few taps.

You can also click the sign displaying as "S" means small or "M" which means medium size and "L" meaning large display.

- Tap "Done" below the Notification Center, when you're finished.

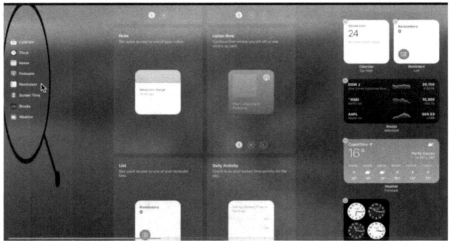

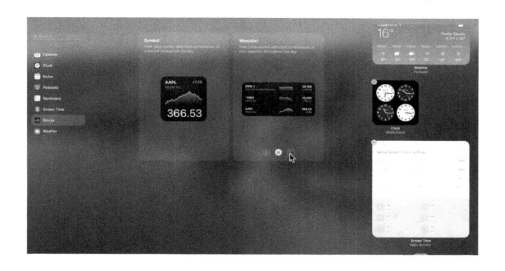

Customizing your Safari start page

Over the years, Safari has a big upgrade in macOS Big Sur, whereas a lot of its adjustments focus on customization.

- Open the Safari start page

- Tap the "Toggle" button beneath your right corner.

Few options will pop up such as Privacy Report, Background Image, Reading List, Favorites, Siri Suggestions and Frequently Visited. There's a checkbox close to each of these options; you can uncheck any of it to take it away from your Safari start page.

Supposing the Background picture is checked/ticked, tap the + button to use another background image using default options or pictures on your Mac.

Note: Safari prevents trackers from following you across websites.

Pinning your favorite conversations in Messages

It is now possible in Big Sur to pin favorite conversations to appear at the up of the pile in your Messages. This would be very useful when you've a small number of people you often talk to and wouldn't want to lose them under the conversation list of threads.

- From your Message, Ctrl-click a conversation at the left-hand corner.
- Tap "Pin"
- The thread would then be moved to the up of your conversation list. Rather than the standard view list displaying the individual's name, photo and content of message, it would display a big picture of them together with the name below, making them differentiated and unique. A total number of nine conversations can be pinned all at once.
- You can also unpin a conversation by right clicking and tap "Unpin."

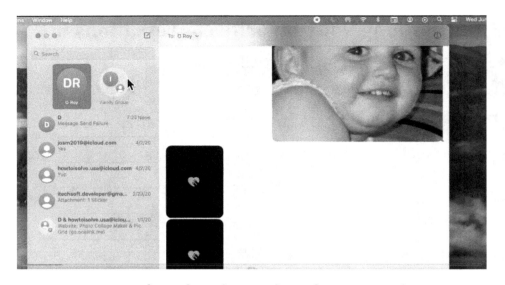

A screenshot showing a pinned conversation

Setting group photos in your Messages

Messages application has additional customizations that are now an innovative concept in Big Sur: images can be set having a lot of people for a particular group. It can be a group member' headshots, a reduction of the name of the group to its main initials, a photo, an emoji, or a Memoji, from the Mac.

You can begin with:

- Ctrl-click a group,
- Tap "Details"
- Here, you can tap "Change Name of Group and Photo." When you tap an emoji or an initial

reduction, the color of the background can also be adjusted and tapping a Memoji enables you to adjust its appearance.

To add a Memoji:

- Click on the app store icon next to the typing text box and see the different imessage options like photos, memoji stickers and message effect which we can browse from the internet using a search keyword.

- Select an image and press the return button from the keyboard to send it

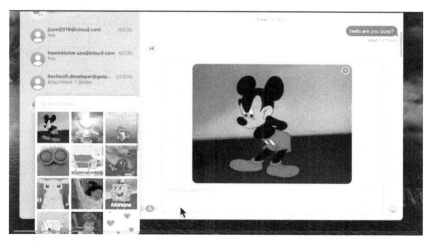

How to create Guide in Map

Within these recent years, Apple has widely enhanced maps making Big Sur not exceptional. One of these significant changes is the institution of Guides. They are a group of places that are related round a theme, like hidden treasures in your town or a huge hiking trail closer to you.

In creating a guide for yourself:

- Go to "Maps"
- Tap "Add Guide" in your sidebar
- Name it
- Navigate to where you wish to add it
- Tap and drag the home's icon from map to guide, and continue doing it for all places you wish to include to guide.

Customizing the app for Reminders

Although Apple's Reminder Application doesn't have a huge adjustment in macOS Big Sur, rather it comes with a few new options of customization that makes it very useful than it previously was.

No. 1 on this list is the ability to reorganize your smart lists. Ordinarily, Today list is usually more projected at the top left corner, but when you wish for another list to occupy this spot instead, drag and drop it in place.

Another adjustment is that you can include an emoji to names appearing on your lists of Reminders:

- Ctrl-click a list,
- Tap "Rename"
- Tap "Edit"
- Then "Emoji & Symbols" on your menu bar to include an emoji.

Adding items to your share sheets

Though share sheets aren't new in the macOS Big Sur, just that they are reformed, with a better view thereby bringing more clarity. For you to customize the items to display on a share sheet:

- Locate a shareable item (like the link of a website or an image)
- Tap the "Share" button or Ctrl-click it
- Tap "Share."
- Tap "More" at the bottom of the share menu to view System Preferences.

- At this point, you can include or remove something on your share menu by tapping the checkbox closer to the items.
- Once you're done, just close System Preferences.

CHAPTER FOUR

FIXING COMMON ISSUES ARISING ON MACOS BIG SUR

In situations whereby issues are arising on macOS Big Sur after the installation of the new update, you'll learn how to fix it here. Apple has tagged macOS Big Sur to be it most radical update to its functioning system over the years, turning such changes into a whole new version.

Bringing out this main milestone in macOS in history happens same time with Apple's MacBook Air (M1, 2020), Mac mini (M1, 2020), and MacBook Pro 13-inch (M1, 2020) all launched newly, whereby all make use of Apple's M1 chip, instead of being driven by Intel hardware.

Such innovative devices come with macOS Big Sur installed already on it, as Apple has declared that the system of operation has been developed from bottom to top to grab the advantage of new hardware.

Therefore, even when you're using an older MacBook or Mac, you should be able to make use of the new system of operation.

If though you're having issues concerning installation, or you have software and hardware that are not working as it supposed to, there are a range of solutions.

One common issue of the macOS Big Sur usually encountered by an individual is the failure to download issue and popping up an error message which says "Installation Failed."

Other issues could be loss of network connection "error messages where they try downloading macOS Big Sur.

This is not all; rather, others may get the error messages seen below such as, "Try again later", and the particular content couldn't be downloaded as at this time", "Installation of macOS could not continue." Installation requires downloading important content.

Various reasons could trigger this issue; maybe a lot of persons are trying at the same time to get the macOS Big Sur downloaded. If you figured that this is the situation, try downloading it at a non-peak time to know if the download would work then. You can as well check the live status of the Apple Server to ensure everything is ok on Apple's end.

There should be a labelled section tagged "macOS Software Update" if you see a green dot, there is no problem, but if you see other colors, it denotes that a problem has occurred while Apple is delivering the update.

Also, it could be that there's not enough storage space on your PC. Normally, downloading macOS can fail if there's not enough storage space accessible on your Mac. To ensure you do:

- Open the "Apple" menu
- Tap on "About This Mac"
- Choose "Storage"

Check to ensure you have enough storage space on your hard drive.

Note: It would require at least 15GB free. But if the storage space is running low:

- Open "Apple" menu
- Tap "About this Mac"
- Go to "Storage"

- Manage and at this same time, free up various disk space here
- It may also require you to switch from a Wi-Fi connection to an Ethernet Cable, to make sure your internet connection is very much reliable.
- In situations whereby you're still finding it difficult to download macOS Big Sur, do well to locate the files you downloaded partially, and a file called "Install macOS 11" on your hard drive. Remove them, and then reboot your Mac and try downloading macOS Big Sur again.
- But if that didn't work, try to open the App Store and click "View My Account" to view whether there's anything in your "unfinished Downloads" section. Maybe you could restart your download from there.
- Lastly, try to log out of the Store to know if it restarts the download.

Fixing "gateway timed out" error when downloading macOS Big Sur

If you have complaints about downloading stopping and your system is popping up a "gateway timed out" even error of "bad gateway."

- Just try to start your Mac in a Safe Mode:
- Press and hold down the Shift key on your keyboard while it boots and try to download and install macOS Big Sur again. Or click on "Apple Support System" and click on "Software Update" also click on "IP Checker and tap "Speedtest" then "Go."

Fixing macOS Big Sur installation problems

Peradventure the issue your macOS Big Sur is having is to install the operating system, first of all, ensure you cross-check on downloading and installing of macOS Big Sur Guide that would help you through the various steps to take to install the new operating system securely.

Firstly, you would want to ensure that you have a Mac that runs macOS Catalina. The following Macs are compatible:

- 12-inch MacBook (2015 and later)
- MacBook Air (2013 and later)
- MacBook Pro (Late 2013 and later)
- Mac mini (2014 and later)
- iMac (2014 and later)
- iMac Pro (all models)
- Mac Pro (2013 and later)

After you've discovered that your Mac is compatible and macOS Big Sur download is completed. At the same time, there's no instruction to continue the installation, and search in your Mac's app folder for a file called 'Install macOS 11'. If you double-tap the file, it should start the installation process.

When you encounter macOS Big Sur issue when the installation is not completed due to insufficient disk space:

- Just restart the Mac and tap Ctrl + R while it's still booting to enter a Recovery mode.
- Choose "Disk boot" to normally boot
- Remove the files that are unnecessary to create more space

If you're setting up your Mac, and the macOS Big Sur is stuck

If after you've installed the macOS Big Sur and your Mac got stuck while setting it up, you have to force it to reboot (i.e. the Mac or a MacBook). Nothing to worry about, the message sent to you for setting up the Mac means that your update is completed, then you wouldn't have to lose any information or get anything damaged while restarting the Mac.

In doing so:

- Turn off you mac and turn it back on

- Long press the "Power" button down for some seconds till your MacBook or Mac is turned off. Hesitate for some seconds, and turn it back on.
- The MacBook or Mac is now expected to boot into macOS Big Sur successfully.
- Maybe, you're stressed with freeing up space on a disk; search for hidden Time Machine files that might seem to be absorbing so much space.

Immediately storage space is freed, and there's now space, try the installation again.

In case you're having a problem with macOS Catalina at the last stage of the installation, and it displays a message error, try to restart your Mac and tap Command + Option + R right on the keyboard when the Mac boots to startup the system for recovery over the web. You can also try Shift + Option + Command + R.

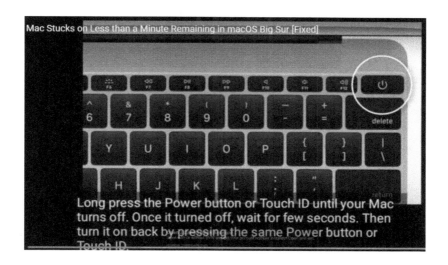

Fixing login issues

If you're having challenges to log into your MacBook or Mac after installation, or if you're battling in a particular spot where you're logging in, log out again and follow the steps below because it might be helpful.

- First of all, try to restart your Mac and press down the Command + S keys on your keyboard as it's booting up
- It will boot up into a command that prompt. Then, enter the following:
- /bin/mount -uw /
- Tap "Enter" from your keyboard. And enter the following:

- rm /var/db/.applesetupdone
- It takes files away and makes it look like you're just beginning Big Sur for the very first time. Nothing to worry about, no important data will be lost. Tap "Enter" and restart your Mac.
- It would then be required of you to create a new admin user account.

What do you do when fans on MacBook are noisy after you update to Big Sur

Several persons had reported that when they updated to macOS Big Sur, their MacBook fans have noticeably become louder.

It may be because your MacBook is working consistently behind the scenes and updating the other operating system as well as updating Application and re-indexing Finder. It may result in the fans kicking in to enable you Keep your MacBook cool. Optimistically, after some hours, your fans would be able to return to normal.

When macOS Big Sur is running slowly, this is how you can fix it.

As soon as macOS Big Sur has been successfully installed on your MacBook or Mac, it may be noticed that your device is now running slower compared to before.

When macOS Big Sur displayed as well a notification showing "Optimizing Your Mac: Performance and Battery Life might be affected till completion," this is, therefore, normal because macOS is doing something behind the scenes that can primarily impact performance.

After maybe a day or so, the Mac is expected to be running as well (if not even better) than before. But if you don't notice any improvement, try to restart your Mac.

One more thing to do is to check and ensure that all your software and application are well updated to the latest version. Because if any of the versions are having issues with Big Sur, it could be lead to slowing down your machine.

If you're making use of a new Mac with Apple's M1 chip, you may be using an application that is not optimized yet. Whereas Apple's Rosetta tool enables the running of application for Intel-based Macs on Apple M1 devices in running Big Sur, you may be having some issues with performance. Look out for the recent versions to find out if an update for M1 Macs has been released.

Also, you can:

- Open "Apple" menu
- Choose "System Preferences"
- From the window that displays, Tap "Users & Groups."
- Choose "Login Items"
- Choose the application you wish to stop from opening during startup and tap the little minus sign beneath the list.
- Also, ensure that all your application is updated.

It's also worth making sure all your apps are updated. Go to the "App Store" to see if there are any updates available, or directly to the website of the app. website.

Also, you can try to restart your Mac to find out if that would help. If it doesn't, force any app that seen to be taking up a lot of RAM to quit. These can be identified by using "Activity Monitor" (in /Applications/Utilities) in establishing the application and procedures are consuming the most RAM or CPU.

To force an item to quit:

- Tap on the "Activity Monitor" list
- Tap the "X" at the left-hand side of the toolbar
- Confirm when prompted that you wish to force-quit.

Fixing issues with macOS Big Sur battery

At some point, you may discover that the battery life of your MacBook is now shorter. The Big Sur is carrying out some underground work to set it up for you, after some hours or a day, you would discover that everything has been resolved and your battery life is normalized.

In case it doesn't, ensure all your application are updated. Also, you can tap on the battery icon at the top menu bar that would display to you the applications and processes that are consuming more battery life. Endeavor to close them up to see if the battery life would improve. If it still doesn't improve, ensure the application in question is updated and check the reason it would be consuming more battery life in the device.

Fixing issues associated with macOS Big Sur mouse

After installing macOS Big Sur and discover your mouse is no longer working fine:

- Open up the "~/Library/Preferences/ directory in finder and choose and delete the following files:
- com.apple.AppleMultitouchMouse.plist
- com.apple.driver.AppleBluetoothMultitouch.mouse. plist
- Alternatively, you can try restarting your Mac to get your mouse working.

Fixing issues with Bluetooth in your Mac

If you're having issues with Bluetooth device, maybe it's not working in your Mac to:

- Open "Finder"
- Tap on "Go" at the top menu,
- Tap "Go to Folder...."
- Type in "/Library/Preferences."
- At this point, a file should display called 'com.apple.Bluetooth.plist '.

- Choose and remove the file (or you can also safe keep it by moving it to a different folder for future use),
- Restart your Mac
- Try to connect your Bluetooth device again.

Fixing issues with macOS Big Sur Wi-Fi

Suppose issues are arising concerning connecting your Mac to the internet, either through Wi-Fi or an Ethernet (wired) connection after the installation has been done. In that case, you can try to restart your Mac while in Safe Mode and find out if you can now connect.

If it works, it then means that there is a problem with an extension or app that you've previously installed. Ensure you have updated all your apps and drivers while being conscious of Apple's future updates.

CHAPTER FIVE

HOW TO SET UP YOUR NEW MAC

It may take about 20min to set up your new Mac, and you'll be directed throughout the process of setting up.

Firstly, take out your Mac from the box, and connect the power cable, including all pertinent peripherals which include pointing devices and keyboards, then press the power button.

Apple's trademark logo will then display on the screen, and you can begin setting up your PC.

This will necessitate you to almost instantly connect a Wi-Fi, therefore ensure you have the necessary credentials ready prepared. Some promptings will then display for you to provide your information like keyboard layout, time zone and if you wish to share anonymous usage data with Apple.

Note: your Mac would require an Apple ID for iCloud, iTunes, App Store, and other purposes and if you already have an existing Apple ID you're using for your device, you can use the same account. But if you don't have, endeavor to create one now.

As soon as you've made it past the initial setup, your Mac will then restart. A clean desktop will display with a row of icons (called the Dock) below screen. You're then ready to start!

The Fundamentals of Using MacOS

Let's begin with the most significant parts when using your Mac.

Desktop and Menu Bar

After your Mac boots up for the first time, it will display the main user interface mechanisms. You'll then find the menu bar at the top of your screen, below is the Dock, and behind your windows, you'll see the desktop.

Similar to various desktop operating systems, macOS makes use of a desktop as its short term workspace where files can be stored. External drives, hard drives and mounted disk images will all display here once connected to your machine. You can then right-click to create new folders and drag to organize your desktop as you desire.

The menu bar fluctuates at the top part of the screen depending on the app presently in emphasis.

The menu in Apple is where you can easily shut-down your machine and information accessible to you relating to your Mac. You can find this under "About This Mac" option.

The menu bar shows app alternatives like File, Help, and Edit etc. At the right-hand side of your menu bar, you'll discover status signs for system and third-party applications. It includes battery meters and Wi-Fi, including applications like Evernote or Shazam.

These items can be rearranged by pressing and holding the Command while at the same time clicking and dragging.

The Dock

It is the nearest equal macOS has to a Windows Start menu. It's often used on the MacBook. The Dock is divided into two namely: Pinned Folders or minimized windows and Shortcuts to applications. The doc can be arranged to display alongside the right edges, bottom or left part of your screen according to System Preferences followed by Dock.

- Go to pinned apps by tapping on them.
- **Note:** Applications that weren't pinned will display as well on the Dock while in use.
- Right-click on any icon to choose if you want to keep in the Dock or not, then drag applications to readjust them. Also, you can drag icons out of the Dock and free it to take them away.

When you drag a file over an application icon and free it, the file in that app would be opened, supposing the application is not compatible with the said file. Dragging an app file into the Dock will include the file into the Dock as a shortcut.

You can find few folders that are pinned and Trash at the other (right-hand) section, Drag whichever folder into the dock to pin it. Files can be taken to the folders by dragging them to move them, the same way you can drag files into Trash to remove them.

Furthermore, if you wish to delete a fixed drive or disk image, drag it and take to the Trash. The Trash can be emptied by right-clicking and selecting "Empty Trash."

Customize the Touch Bar

You may not like the way the touch bar comes out of the box. Therefore, you would want to customize that as well. To do this:

- Go to "System Preferences"
- Click "Keyboard"
- Click the "Customize Control Strip" Button
- Drag the buttons you want to show on the default view of the touch bar below the display
- Position them where you want on the touch bar

Show Battery Percentage

By default, the percentage of battery is not visible.

To enable this:

- Click on the battery indicator on the menu bar
- Select "Show Percentage."

The Finder

Just like we have Windows Explorer, Finder is a default macOS file management application. It enables you to browse your hard drives through, including other devices that are connected.

There are various elements you can find in the Finder window, under which you can toggle the View menu bar items:

- **Tab bar:** It automatically displays and covers anytime you open a new tab inside Finder (Cmd + T).
- **Path bar:** It shows the way to the current folder below the screen.
- **Status bar**: Displays the number of items in the form of a list in a place and disk space availability.
- **Sidebar:** It's a list of frequently-used or preferred locations at the left-hand side.
- **Preview:** It's a preview pane expanded at the right-hand side of your window.
- Your Sidebar is mostly useful because it can be customized to show your preferred location. Right-

click and select "Remove" from the Sidebar to delete any entry.

To permanently include a folder into a sidebar, click and drag the folder into it.

Scroll down to the section of the device to view presently mounted disks and volumes below that you can find locations of shared network and tags. To remove or include sections, tap "Finder" then "Preferences" in your menu bar above your screen.

Finder uses the main toolbar to show controls that are common like forward and back. To customize a Finder, right-click on your toolbar.

You can remove or add buttons and shortcuts, also rearranging of fields like the search bar. The search bar appears to be visible by default wherein it can be used to search the whole Mac or just the folder you're presently viewing.

Finder supports "copy" (Cmd + C) and "paste" (Cmd + V) certainly not "cut".

Move substitutes cut on macOS. For you to "cut" a particular file, you must endeavor to copy it first, before moving it (Cmd + Option + V). When you right-click and tap the Option key, you'll find "Paste" change to "Move."

The Spotlight

It is the identity of Mac's search engine, displaying in a floating window each time you tap Cmd + Space. Just input your query and macOS will immediately respond with context-sensitive results. Press "Enter" to display the top results, or scroll over what the Spotlight has discovered until you see whatever you're searching for.

This search tool that is handy works not only for finding files but as an app launcher as well. Just by typing, you can:

- Find emails, files, documents, folders, notes, messages etc.
- Open apps and other functions

Execute elementary calculations

- Exchange measurements, currencies including other units
- Require access to suggested websites, Wikipedia entries, definitions, etc.
- Use regular language for filtering results

Applications

Most apps you've downloaded from the internet will first display showing disk image (DMG) files. Click twice a DMG to open it, and it will display macOS as a read-only drive. Drag the app (APP) file to your Apps folder to install it. Deleting the APP file from this folder will completely remove the app from your system.

Several applications make use of a packaged installer (PKG) that is similar to how applications are installed on Windows. Run the PKG file and follow the promptings on the screen. A lot of PKG installers use the packaged uninstallers to take away the app. Though these are just the basics, processes are involved in installing and removing of Mac software.

Another major technique of installing Mac software is using the Mac Application Store. It is an app that enables you to achieve the installation process.

- Open "Mac App Store"
- Log in, using your Apple ID
- Locate an application you wish to install

- Tap on "Get" or the price of the item; it all depends on if the application would attract charges or not.
- This application can be deleted as every other regular application.

Note: When you're installing certain third-party apps, it may be prompted by the Gatekeeper that you cannot proceed with the installation, the reason is that the source isn't trusted. Therefore the app developer hasn't applied to Apple to get a developer license, and this is vital for macOS to trust any new software.

To pass through this protection stage:

- Click to dismiss the early dialog and move to "System Preferences."
- Click "Security & Privacy"
- Then tap "Open Anyway" close to the bottom of your screen.

System Preferences

Everything you can locate in system preferences can be pretty much configured, which is by default, pinned to the Dock. It can therefore be accessed with the use of the little silver cog icon, or by right-clicking the icon to go directly to a particular section.

Note: You may find more or few options below your system preferences panel, depending on your Mac model and its attributes.

If you intend to adjust something on your PC, this should be the first thing you're supposed to change. All beginning from including a new user account up to changing trackpad sensitivity, to show resolution and security settings. The search bar located at the top can also be used to easily find a particular preference pane or click view to toggle on alphabetic sorting.

It would be best if you took some time to get yourself use to the very common sections. Some tweaks you may need to make shortly after you've started using your new Mac are as follows:

- Changing your wallpaper in Screen Saver and Desktop
- Changing the behavior, size and alignment of the Dock
- Learning and adjusting gesture controls in Trackpad

- Adding your social media account and new email in internet Accounts
- Set a backup location using Time Machine
- Do not also forget that you can use the Spotlight in searching for any of these preference panes with the Cmd + Space keyboard shortcut.

Notifications and Today Screen

Tap on the three-line icon at the top right corner of your screen to view Notification Center and Today screen. Also, you can swipe with your two fingers from the right edge of the trackpad, or you can set up hot corners to enable easy triggering of this feature.

The "Today screen" is an area meant for widgets, and these are a little piece of information and cooperating elements linking to your other applications. Scroll below of your list and click "Edit" to see your widgets that are available.

You can drag them to rearrange them, then tap on the green + or red - symbols to include or take away widgets.

If an app is sending you notifications, you will get a request wherein you can either approve or deny. Notifications coming in would display at the top right of your screen, below the menu bar. Notification permissions can be revoked or customized in System preferences then Notifications.

Gestures and Navigation

When you're making use of a trackpad, either using a MacBook or Apple's Magic Trackpad accessory, you'll then have access to a variety of gestures on macOS. Gestures activate some features and help to speed up navigation.

These gestures can be customized, and some close example videos can be viewed in "System Preferences" then "Trackpad."

Here, the scroll behavior can be adjusted with two-finger drag, enable to tap (so you wouldn't have to diminish the trackpad fully), adjusting gestures for swiping among desktops (i.e. horizontal three-finger drag).

Several recent MacBooks has "Force Touch trackpads," which is same fundamental technology supporting 3D Touch on an iPhone. This enables you to press slightly, rather than tapping regularly. You can immensely speed up your communications with macOS through having a few simple Mac keyboard shortcuts. Some that are useful to start with are as follows:

- Copy: Cmd + C
- Paste: Cmd + V
- Move (after copying): Cmd + Option + V
- App Switcher: Cmd + Tab
- Screenshot: Cmd + Shift + 3 (captures the whole screen; other ways can also be used to take screenshots)

- Spotlight: Cmd + Space
- Siri: Cmd + Space (hold)
- New Tab (Finder, Safari, and more): Cmd + T

AirPlay and AirDrop

AirDrop is Apple's branded wireless file distributing technology. It can be used to send files among iOS devices and Mac computers such as the iPad and iPhone.

- Go to "Finder"
- Tap on "AirDrop" at the sidebar to view a list of available recipients. When you're expecting to get a file through your Mac, ensure this screen is opened.

Virtually everything can be shared from the Mac using the AirDrop. The fastest way this can be done is:

- Right-click on any file or a link
- Tap "Share"
- Click "AirDrop"

You can as well use the "Share" button developed into many Mac apps such as Notes and Safari.

AirPlay is Apple's branded wireless flowing technology. Audios or videos (even both) can be sent to an AirPlay receiver such as an Apple TV by tapping on the AirPlay icon (underneath) in the menu bar above the screen. Media can as well be sent to receivers while using AirPlay icon when you can possibly access it in some other applications, like Spotify and iTunes.

Tap on AirPlay icon to allow mirroring that sends your Mac's screen to an AirPlay headset according to your preferences. It is perfect for photos sharing and presentations, but the outcome would depend on the interface and network speed.

Also, you may prefer to bring out your Mac's sounds to AirPlay device by selecting them as Output devices in "System Preferences" then "Sound."

Siri

Just as Siri is on iPhone device, that's how Siri is like on a Mac. By pressing and holding the "Cmd + Space" shortcut, it's possible to request Siri to locate your files, get information from the internet, call people or even send messages or email, all from the Mac desktop.

For instance, you can request Siri queries through everyday languages, such as:

- "Display the PDFs I last opened this week".

- "Remind me to be at the glossary store tomorrow".

Using some queries, they can be dragged and pinned to the Today Screen and automatically, they'll update based on recent data. E.g. sports fittings, stock data etc.

CHAPTER SIX

ICLOUD AND MACOS

It is necessary to understand iCloud because you'll certainly locate iCloud all around macOS.

iCloud Defined

iCloud is a common name for Apple's cloud services online. It appears before other supplementary services such as iCloud Music Library or iCloud Drive. It mainly shows that a particular service's information is saved online, in the cloud.

It's not all iCloud services that require iCloud storage. For instance, iCloud Music Library is seen as a cloud-based library meant for Apple subscribers on Music, therefore, ensures the maintenance of the same contents in the library across various devices requiring zero storage space online or otherwise unless you wish to save something in particular offline.

Storage Space

Apple offers 5GB space for free for each Apple ID, irrespective of the fact that you an Apple TV, iPhone, or a brand-new MacBook. You can locate this under your recent storage allocation in "System Preferences" then "iCloud."

You'll also have to consider upgrading the storage in the long run.

For upgrading your storage space:

- Launch "System Preferences"

- Click "iCloud."

- Click "Account Details"

- Select an upgrade.

iCloud On your Mac

In macOS, you will locate a smorgasbord of the features of iCloud made accessible to you of which many can be turned on or off in System Preferences then iCloud.

iCloud Drive is a platform for cloud storage platform. Files could be uploaded to the cloud and can then be accessed on a different Apple device, without having limitations on the file type or how regularly it's been accessed. All you've to do is to ensure that the size of the file is within 50GB.

Several applications pull and push data within Apple's servers, as well as Reminders, Safari, Calendars, Mail and Contacts. These services require no space for storage on iCloud, but using the service as a go-between for keeping all Mac as well as iOS devices synchronizing together.

ICloud.Com

There's a web frontend in iCloud.com that enables the assessment of a particular service from whichever device which includes basics such as Notes, Mail, Calendars and Contacts. Additionally, it holds the "Find My iPhone" service that functions especially when locating your Mac, Pictures to view "iCloud Photo Library", including a friendly web version of iCloud Drive.

You can as well discover iWork for iCloud applications here, including Keynote, Numbers and Pages. These are examples of Apple's iWork Suite that are web-based that can be used to work on several documents you've selected to have in the cloud or new ones can be created.

This frontend web is mostly useful as a webmail service for iCloud mail, help in tracking your friends and devices also to work on documents remotely.

CHAPTER SEVEN

MAINTENANCE AND BACKUPS ON MACOS

Speaking in general, maintaining macOS is not actively done but by running updates and safely keeping of your machine backed up.

macOS Updates

macOS brings updates through the "Mac App Store." For significant system downloads including firmware updates, security fixes, and version of first-party Apple software that is new:

- click on "Apple" at the top left of your screen
- Launch the "App Store" application
- Tap the "Updates" tab.

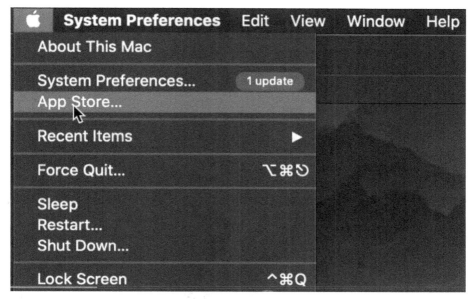

Whichever third-party applications you install from your Mac App Store will as well get updates in this way. Applications you've installed from the internet or via other ways will need manual updating. A lot of apps automatically will inform you of subsequent updates and request if they can be downloaded and installed for you.

Backing Up With Time Machine

The Time Machine is known as a solution on Apple for automatic backup. It usually works when using an external hard drive. Nevertheless, you can designate network places if you wish. To begin this, plug in a blank external hard drive having at least enough space as that of your Mac's system drive. Enough space is preferable because you'll have to scrutinize a bigger archive of backups.

While your drive is connected:

- Go to "System Preferences"
- Click "Time Machine"
- Tap "Select Backup Disk"

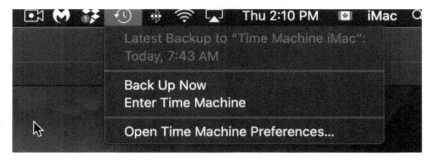

Identify the drive you wish to use in backing up the Mac. It will remove all the contents. Therefore you may wish to create a demarcation that is if you want to store other files on the same drive.

With the specification of a disk, Time Machine starts backing up the Mac. Each time this hard drive is connected, Time Machine will set in while creating a backup.

Note: It wouldn't at every time back up everything, but duplicates the modifications while creating a browsable snapshot from your computer at a particular point in time.

Restoring Mac from Time Machine

In a situation whereby your drive is full, the old backups would be deleted first.

You can decide to browse the backups you need anytime by linking the Time Machine Hard drive, and tapping the "Time Machine" icon at the menu bar and choosing "Enter Time Machine."

The reason for this backup is for restoring your Mac to its original position in case anything goes wrong, e.g. failure of the operating system or hardware or moving to a new Mac entirely also important to secure your Mac when you travel.

macOS Maintenance

Babysitting your Mac isn't necessary, rather there're some maintenance forms that are fundamental and you should endeavor to remember to carry out regularly to enable your machine constantly running smoothly. Interestingly, the most apparent one that helps in maintaining a decent apparatus of free space.

The Mac will, therefore, experience issues regarding performance when its space is running low. The operating system and other third-party applications solely rely on free space that is usable for consistent operating. Or possibly, try maintaining a basic minimum of 10GB of space on the Mac all the time.

When using the Management Storage Application:

- Go to Applications
- Click Utilities, and then you'll find precisely the file taken up most of the space by tapping different categories. The Store in iCloud characteristics allows

the automatic downloading and uploading of files to iCloud as required.

Store in iCloud

You can automatically enable the feature of Empty Trash if you choose to, whereby items would be permanently erased from your trash after every 30 days. Furthermore, tap on the "Review Files" button to view a breakdown of your biggest and files that were used last on your Mac. Here, you can trash what is no longer needed.

The issue about Troubleshooting in MacOS

Issues from time to time would arise since your Mac isn't invulnerable to problems. Therefore you should be ready to prevent such issues and ensure everything is working fine as at when due. This is why it is very important to create frequent backups (as earlier discussed).

Boot Modes

When you hold a particular combination of keys when starting the Mac, it can enter a particular boot mode.

This help to troubleshoot the Mac, run hardware diagnostics or install other functional systems.

1. Apple Diagnostics results

To shut-down, the Mac, tap your power button and instantly press and hold the combinations required. Some of the boot modes you have to memorize are:

- D to enter the Hardware Diagnostic mode to examine the Mac for the possible problem when using Apple's online tool.
- Option (Alt) to list all the bootable volumes and automatically bypass the launching of macOS.
- Shift to start in Safe mode, ideal if you're having problems starting your Mac.
- Cmd + R to enter into a Recovery mode, and ideal for fixing drive issues as well as reinstallation of macOS.

2. PRAM And SMC

Certain challenges can be resolved only when you reset your Mac's Parameter Random Access Memory (PRAM) and System Management Controller (SMC). They play a vital role to keep the Mac running effortlessly, whether it recalls the date and time or the controlling natural elements such as LEDs and fans.

Think differently and be Comfortable With your MacOS

macOS can be easily accessible. Though you might find it difficult to break into the operating system, it is as a result of safety measures put in place by Apple to safeguard the device. As soon as you've modified the layout of your keyboard, gesture-based navigation and of course Apple's method of doing everything, macOS would become a reliable and productive platform where you could spend so much time without even noticing.

CHAPTER EIGHT

NAVIGATIONS IN MACOS

Getting started with macOS

Even if you're a novice in a computer or only new to macOS operating system, it's essential to understand the fundamentals of using your personal computer. In case it's stressing you out, not to worry! You'll be taken through it through a step by step procedure and be shown some of the vital basic things you have to know, such as working with your desktop, turning off your PC or Opening and Closing windows.

The desktop

As soon as your PC has finished starting up, what you'll see displaying at first is the "Desktop." You can consider the desktop as your main workspace on your computer. At this point, your files can be viewed and managed; you can open apps, access the internet and perform other tasks.

Tap the different interactive buttons below to get used to your desktop.

Working with applications

Applications also called a program is a software type that enables you to start and finish a task on your computer. macOS offers so many apps you can make use of. For instance, if you wish to browse the internet, Safari can be used, which is one of the built-in web browsers. An easy way of opening an app is by clicking its icon on the Dock.

For you to open an app:

- Use your mouse and tap an app icon on the Dock.
- The app will display in a new window.
- When you can't seem to find the app you want, tap the "Spotlight" icon at the top right corner of your screen and input the name of the app using your keyboard in searching for it.

Working with windows

Each time you open an app, file or even folder, it will display in a new window. It's possible to have numerous items opened at the same time in various windows. Since you'll be making use of windows at almost all the time, it's very necessary to understand how to switch between open windows, closing windows, when you're through with them, moving and resizing windows.

Parts of a window

You'll find three buttons at the upper left corner of every window you open.

- Tapping the "Red" button will close a window.
- Tapping the "Yellow" button will help minimize a window, therefore keeping it from view. It will then be minimized to the Dock. You can now tap the icon for that window on the Dock to make it reappear.
- Tapping the "Green" button will help maximize the window, making it appear larger. Then you can tap it again to go back to take the window to its original size.

Moving a window

- By tapping and dragging the top of a window to move it to a preferred location on your screen. If you're through, release your mouse.
- The window then will display on the new place.

Resizing a window

- Hover your mouse through the lower right corner of a window,
- Tap and drag your mouse to view your window smaller or larger.
- Once you're through, free your mouse.
- Automatically, the appearance of the window will be resized.

Quitting applications

Different the Microsoft Windows whereby when you close a window automatically quits an app, the macOS doesn't automatically do that. The app will continue to run in the background even when the window is not opened. To find out whether an app is still running, find a little black dot beneath the icon on the Dock.

To enable your PC to run smoothly, you should endeavor to quit an app when you're through with it. To do this, tap the icon on the Dock to change to the app, and tap the app name at the top left corner of your screen and choose Quit from your menu that displays.

Note that you may not be able to quit "Finder" because macOS need Finder to run smoothly continuously.

You can as well quit an app by tapping Command + Q on the keyboard. It is an example showing keyboard shortcut and would be covered in the course of macOS keyboard shortcuts lesson.

Shutting down your computer

If you're through using your PC, it's very important you properly shut it down. But if you wish to stop using it in the meantime, you can put it to sleep mode.

To shut down macOS:

- Tap the "Apple" icon at the top left corner of your screen,
- Tap "Shut Down..."

Restarting and Sleep mode

If you notice other options close to Shut Down command, you'll see other options like restart or sleep mode. For instance, when your PC is now becoming slow or not responding, you can select the Restart option to turn it off and on quickly.

Also, you can put your PC to sleep by tapping sleep mode under the same options. This mode helps to turn off your computer processes while remembering the apps and files that are opened. It enables the computer to start up very quickly, especially when you don't have the time to wait for the operating system and apps to load all over again.

Note: Your PC may automatically go to "Sleep mode when you've not used it for more than a few minutes.

You can as well close the lid of your laptop to put it to sleep mode.

How to wake your computer from Sleep mode

You'll have to wake your computer if it's in sleep mode. To do this, tap your mouse or tap any key on your keyboard.

CHAPTER NINE

HOW TO WORK WITH FOLDERS AND FILES

File basics

You would enjoy using your computer when you understand how you can work with folders and files because it is a vital part of using your computer.

As soon as you know how folders and files work, you can be able to use them at all times. Here, you would learn the basics of how you can work with files, as well as how to open them, move them into folders including deleting them.

Understanding what a file is

There are numerous types of files you can make use of. For instance, Digital Music, Videos, Photos and Microsoft Word documents, all various type of files. You may as well consider a file to be a digital version of a real-world thing that you can interact with using your computer. If you use the various app, you'll usually be able to create, edit or create files. Usually, files are signified by an icon.

Understanding what a folder is

The folder is very useful to macOS because it helps to organize your files. Various files can be put inside a particular folder, just as you would add documents inside a real folder.

macOS uses folders to help you organize files. You can put files inside a folder, just like you would put documents inside a real folder.

What is a Finder?

Your files can be viewed and organized and your folders with the use of a built-in app called Finder.

To access Finder:

- Tap the "Finder" icon at the Dock, or click twice without hesitation any folder on the desktop. A new Finder window would display

- At this point, you're prepared to begin working with files and folders.

- From the "Finder", click twice without hesitation any folder to open it.

You can now view all the files you've saved in that particular folder.

- You can as well tap a location in the Sidebar at the left to go to another folder.

Note: the name of the current folder would display, and you can view it at the top of your Finder window.

If for instance, the Sidebar is not noticeable at the left side of your Finder Window, choose "View" then "Show Sidebar" from your Menu bar.

To open a file

You can open a file with two basic ways.

Locate a file on the computer and click it twice (such action would open the file as it is in the app).

- Click to open an application,
- From the App, Open a file.
- As soon as the app is opened, then you can now go to the "File" menu close to the top left corner of your screen.
- Choose "Open."

Moving and deleting files

When you start using your PC, more and more files will be collected from time to time and can make it difficult to locate a particular file you need at a particular time. Luckily, macOS enables you to move various files to different folders as well as deleting the ones that are no longer needed.

How to move a file

You can easily move your files from a particular location to another. For instance, you may have a file on the desktop you wish to take to Documents folder:

- Tap and drag the particular file to the preferred location
- Free your mouse.
- You'll discover that the file will display in the new location.
- **Note:** Similar technique can be used to move a folder entirely. Also take note that when you move a folder, all the files in the particular folder will move with the said folder.

How to create a new folder

- Choose "File" within a Finder
- Click "New Folder" from your Menu bar close to the top left corner of your screen
- Also, you can tap Command + N from your keyboard.
- The folder you want to create will now display
- Input a preferred name for the folder
- Tap "Enter"

At this point, the new folder has been created; you can then move your files to the new folder.

How to rename a file or folder

You can choose to change the name of a folder or file. A distinctive name can be given to enable you to recall easier the type of information that is saved into the folder or file.

- Tap the "Folder" or "File"
- Hesitate for about a second,
- Tap again. A text filed you can edit would display
- Input the desired name using your keyboard
- Tap "Enter" (you would notice that the name has changed).

How to delete a file or folder

If you no longer have a use for a file, the file can be deleted. By deleting the file, you've succeeded in moving it to the Trash. Peradventure, you need to use the file again; you can go to the Trash and move the file back to where it was before. But if you're sure you wouldn't need it again, you can delete the file permanently when you empty your Trash.

Tap and drag a folder or file to the Trash icon on the Dock. Alternatively, you can choose the file and tap "Command + Delete" on your keyboard.

To delete a file permanently, tap and hold and hold the Trash icon, and choose "Empty Trash." All the files in your Trash will be deleted permanently.

Note: When you delete a folder, all the files in that particular folder will be deleted.

Choosing to move multiple files

As you now understand the basics, below are some tips that would help you know how you can move your files even faster.

Selecting more than a single file

Maybe you're seeing your files displaying like icons; you can tap and drag your mouse to put a box around the files you wish to choose. Once you're through, free your mouse; your files will then be selected. A particular number of files can be copied, moved or deleted at once.

To choose particular files from a folder:

- Tap and hold the Command key on your keyboard
- Tap the particular files you wish to select.

To choose a group of files adjacent in a folder:

- Tap the first file
- Tap and hold the "Shift" key on your keyboard,
- Tap the last file. (all the files from the first to last would be selected)

If for instance, you wish to choose all the files in a folder at once:

- Launch the Folder in "Finder"
- Tap Command + A key (All the files in the particular folder would be selected).

If you're still finding it difficult at this time to work with folders and files, you've nothing to worry about. Just like other things, it requires constant practice to work with folders and files because you'll become used to it as you continue to use your computer consistently.

CHAPTER TEN

USING SHORTCUTS

If there's any folder or file you frequently use, you can save yourself some stress when you create a shortcut on your desktop. Rather than navigating to your various folders or files all the time you want to use them, just double-click to open them. A shortcut usually has a little arrow at the lower-left corner of the folder or file's icon.

Note: when you create a shortcut, it doesn't create a duplicate of the said folder. It's just a way of accessing it faster. And when you delete a particular shortcut, the real file or folder it contains will not be deleted. Also take note that when you copy a shortcut into a flash drive, it will not function. But if you wish to take a particular file or folder with you, go to the real location of the folder or file before you can copy it to a flash drive.

How to create a shortcut

- Go to where the folder is located on your computer.
- Tap and hold the Command and Option keys on your keyboard

- Tap and drag a folder to your desktop
- A shortcut to the folder or file will display on your desktop.
- Observe and see the arrow located at the lower-left corner of the icon.
- You can then double-click the shortcut you've created to open the file or folder anytime you want to.

Finding Files on Your Computer

Locating your files

Previously, we dwelt on how your folders and files can be organized. Nevertheless, there are times when you might be having difficulty in locating a particular file or folder. If this is the situation, relax! The file might still be in your computer somewhere and can be located with a few good techniques. Some of these techniques you can use to locate a file would be revealed here.

Common places to look for files

When you're having issues with locating a particular file, you have a good chance to locate it in one of the places below.

Current Items: If you edited a needed file recently, it's possible to look for it in the list of your Recent Items. For you to access it:

- Tap the "Apple" icon at the top left corner of your screen

- Choose "Recent Items" from your menu.

- A list containing recent files and apps that were used would display. When you see the file you want, tap on it to open.

Downloads: Normally, your downloaded files are placed in a particular folder, called "Downloads" folder. And if you have trouble locating your downloaded files from the internet, just as a picture attached to an email message, it is the first place you're expected to look at. Find and tap the Download folder located at the right side of the Dock. Then a downloaded list of files would display at the top of the folder.

Default folders: In a situation whereby you didn't identify a location while saving a file, macOS will then place a specific file type into a default folder. For instance, when you're search for a Microsoft Word doc, locate it in the Documents folder. And when you're searching for a photo, try the folder for Pictures. Much of the folders can be accessed from the Sidebar at the left side of the Finder window.

Trash: When you mistakenly delete a file, it would still be in the Trash. Just tap the "Trash" icon on the Dock for you to open it.

After locating the file, you want to restore, tap and drag it to your desktop or another folder entirely.

Searching for files

If for instance, you downloaded a few photos recently that were attached to an email, but you're not sure at the moment where the files can be found on your computer. When you're having difficulty in locating a file, you can search for it. By searching, it enables you to locate for a file on your computer.

You can do this:

- Tap the "Spotlight" icon at the top right corner of your screen
- Input the name of the file or keywords in a search box. The results of the search would display as you enter it.
- Just tap a particular folder or file to open it.

Additionally, you can tap "Show All in Finder" above the results to view the location of your files in a new Finder window.

Tips for locating files

Are you still having issues with locating a file you want, here are various additional tips that would help you.

Try various searching terms. But if you're making use of the search option, endeavor to use a different term in your search tab. For instance, when you're searching for a particular Microsoft Word doc, search for a few various names of files you may have used while saving the doc.

- Open the previous app used in editing the File.
- If you're sure of the app you used in editing a file,
- Open the particular app and choose File

- Tap "Open Recent" from the menu. (The File would display on the list of files recently edited).
- You can rename and move the File after locating it. You can choose to move it to a folder related to it so you can easily locate it sometime in the future. If for example, the file type is a photo, you can choose to move it to your folder for Pictures. Also, you can give it a file name that is related that you can easily remember.

CHAPTER ELEVEN

COMMON COMPUTER TASKS

Sometimes, learning how you can use a computer can seem overwhelming. Luckily, various computer skills are common and will work similarly in almost all situations. After learning how to use the skills, you can be able to carry out different tasks in your computer. Some commands are common and can be used in almost all apps, such as undo, cut, paste and how to right-click with your Mouse in macOS.

The menu bar

After opening an app, you can now use the Menu bar at the top left corner of your screen. Every menu has some commands that can carry out a particular action in a program. Whereas every app is distinct, various commands are common and can work the same way irrespective of the app you're making use of. Anytime you open a program for the first time, endeavor to tap these menus to view the various options.

Application menu commands

You can locate the app menu at the right of the Apple icon at the menu bar. It would display the app name that's presently opened.

File menu commands

Locate the menu of the File at the right of the app menu. The file menu usually has the same command type. For instance, new files can be created, existing ones can be opened, or the current ones can be saved.

Right-clicking the Mouse

A lot of tasks would require that you right-click using your trackpad or Mouse. It usually enables you to access a menu having convenient shortcuts, which varies depending on the type of app you're using. In macOS, to right-click is by default disabled but you can easily activate the feature.

To enable right-clicking:

- Tap the "Apple" icon at the top left corner of your screen
- Choose "System Preferences" at the Apple menu

- When the System Preferences displays, choose the category of the Mouse.

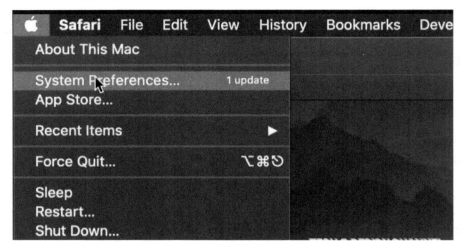

- Check the box close to Secondary tap. The right-clicking would be enabled. When you're using a mouse lacking a clear right button (like the "Magic Mouse"), you can right-click by tapping close to the right side of your Mouse.

Other ways of right-clicking

If your right-clicking is not enabled, you can therefore perform a click secondarily (or right-tap) anytime you like on your Mac. Tap and hold the Ctrl key from your keyboard and tap your mouse.

You can click a trackpad with two-finger to right-click if you have it. Alternatively, you can:

- Go to "System Preferences"
- Click "Trackpad" to select other options for right-clicking on the trackpad.

How to copy, paste and cut

A lot of apps permit you to copy items from one particular location and past them in another location. For instance, when you're working on a word processor, you may copy text and paste it to avoid repeating the typing of the same thing over again. If there's anything you wish to move from one location to another, cut and paste instead.

To copy and paste:

- Choose the particular item you wish to copy.
- Right-click your mouse and choose "Copy" from the menu that display.
- You can as well tap Command + C on the keyboard.
- Find and click twice the preferred location for the item.
- Choose "Paste."
- You can as well tap Command + V on the keyboard.

99

- The file would be copied to a new location.

The item will be copied to the new location. You would notice that the original text you copied has not been changed or moved.

To cut and paste:

- Choose the particular item you wish to cut.
- Right-click your mouse and choose "Cut" from the displayed menu. You can as well tap "Command + X" from your keyboard.
- Find and right-click the preferred location for the particular item,
- Choose "Paste."
- You can as well tap "Command + V" from your keyboard.

The item will be pasted, or moved, to the new location. In our example, we used the cut and paste commands to move the second paragraph above the first paragraph.

How to copy and paste files:

- The Copy, Paste and Cut commands can also be used to perform various tasks on your computer. For instance, when you want to duplicate a copy of a file, the file can be copied from a particular folder to another.

- Right-click the said file and choose Copy from the menu that would display. Also, you can tap Command + C from your keyboard.

- Find and right-click a new location and choose Paste. Also, you can tap Command + V from your keyboard.

- Your duplicate Copy of the file would display. You would notice that the Original Copy of the file has not been moved or changed but remain the way it is and where it was. Also take note that if there are any changes you're making on the original Copy of your file, certainly, it wouldn't update copies of that file. Be careful to note that when you copy a file is not the same thing as when you create a shortcut.

Undoing changes

Assuming, you're working on a particular document and unintentionally deleted some text. Luckily, it's not for you to start retyping everything that you unintentionally deleted! Various apps enable you to undo the most recent action if you've made a mistake as such.

- Tap the "Edit" menu on your Menu bar and choose "Undo." Alternatively, you can tap Command + Z from the keyboard. This Command can be used continuously to undo numerous changes at a stretch.
- Take note that the Undo command may work in nearly all situations but not in every condition. For instance, if you've emptied your trash by permanently deleting a file, this action cannot be reverted.

Now that you're aware of the commands commonly used, which you can use in almost all apps on your computer. As earlier mentioned in this book, there are a series of shortcuts on your keyboard that can be used to perform these commands faster than you can imagine. This will be discussed during keyboard shortcut lessons on macOS.

Adjusting your settings

At a particular point in time, you would want to change the settings of your computer. For instance, you may wish to adjust the background of your desktop or even modify the internet settings. These settings can be possible from your System Preferences.

How to open System Preferences

- Tap the "Apple" icon at the top left corner of your screen,
- Choose "System Preferences."
- The window of the System Preferences would display
- Just tap your preferred settings to modify it.
- The System Preferences window will appear. Click the desired setting to adjust it.
- Alternatively, you can tap the "System Preferences" icon on the Dock to view these settings at whichever time.

Other important settings

Some settings are not accessible via System Preferences. For instance, if you wish to customize how your Finder Window would display:

- Go to Finder
- Tap Preferences

If you wish to customize your settings for a different app like Safari, tap the name of the program in the Menu bar and choose "Preferences..."

If you wish to adjust the ways items displays on your desktop, right-click your desktop and choose "Show View Options" from the menu that would display.

At this point, you can now adjust the icon's size in your desktop, enlarge the whole size of the text while you make other changes.

CHAPTER TWELVE

UNDERSTANDING USER ACCOUNTS

What are user accounts?

User Account is an avenue of signing in to your computer. Ordinarily, your Mac has an already existing user account that it's required of you to create while setting your computer. If you're planning of sharing your computer with other persons, a separate account can be created for every individual.

Why have separate user accounts

Here, you may be thinking about why you would need separate user accounts. For instance, you're sharing a particular computer with different people, maybe your office place or your family. User account permits everyone to individually save their files, preferences including settings while avoiding affecting other computer users. If you're just starting your computer, you can select what account you wish to use.

Administrator, Standard, and Managed accounts

Before creating a new user account, you must know the various types.

Administrator's Account: It's a special account used when you're making changes on your system settings or when managing other accounts. They can access all the setting on your computer. Each computer should at least have one Administrator's account, but if you're an already existing owner, then you should have a password to the account.

Standard Account: It is the basic accounts you can use for regular tasks every day. As a Standard account user, anything you wish to do can be done, such as personalizing the desktop and running software.

Managed Accounts: These are accounts that are specific to have parental controls. A managed account can be created for every child, and go to "Parental Controls" settings in "System Preferences" to set the internet boundaries, time limitations and so on. Also, it is possible to convert a Standard account into a Managed account when you enable parental controls.

Usually, it's more secured to be signed into a Standard account instead of an Administrator's account. When you sign in as an Administrator, an unauthorized user can easily adjust your computer. As a result of this, you may wish to create a personal Standard account, even while you're not sharing your computer with someone else. And you can still possibly make changes at the Administrator-level; all you've to do is to provide the Administrator's Password.

Creating a new user account:

- Launch the "Apple" icon to go to "System Preferences."
- Choose "Users and Groups"
- Find the "Lock" icon at the lower-left corner of your window. It should either be closed or opened.
- When it is closed, you'll have to click on it and input your Password to make adjustments.
- Tap "Unlock" when you're through
- Tap the "button" having the plus sign (+) to start to create a new account.

- Select the type of account from the drop-down menu.
- Input your "Full Name" and "Password" used for the new account (your Account name will automatically display).
- In the field for verification, input your Password for a second time (You can choose to input a hint for Password if you wish to enable you remembers it)
- Tap "Create User" when you're through

Switching to a different account:

- Tap the "Apple" icon,
- Choose "Log Out"
- A screen for signing in will display. Enter your preferred username and password
- Tap "Enter" (Note that there is some macOS version that would require you to choose the user account before you can type your password).

CHAPTER THIRTEEN

KEYBOARD SHORTCUTS IN MACOS

Understanding what is meant by keyboard shortcuts?

Keyboard shortcuts are keys or a combination of keys you can press on your keyboard to perform a variety of tasks. Using keyboard shortcuts is often faster than using a mouse because you can keep both hands on the keyboard. Keyboard shortcuts are also universal, which means you can use many of the same shortcuts in a variety of applications. For example, you can use the same shortcut to copy and paste text in a word processor and a web browser.

Using shortcuts

A lot of keyboard shortcuts need you to tap two or more keys in a particular order. For instance, when you want to carry out a shortcut "Command + X", it would be required that you tap and hold your" Command" Key, at the same time tap the X key and then free.

Take note that the Option, Control and Command keys would be used in performing a lot of shortcuts. It is located close to the bottom left corner of the keyboard.

When you're not using a Mac keyboard, the Option or Command keys may not be accessible. What it means is that you may have to experiment using key combinations to carry out certain keyboard shortcuts.

Working with text

The keyboard shortcuts below are very useful, especially when you're working with text in email apps, word processors and so on. It can be used to perform repeated tasks that are common such as to copy and paste the text.

- Command + X: Totally "Cut" a text selected.
- Command + C: To "Copy" a text selected.
- Command + V: To "Paste" a text cut or copied.
- Command + A: To "Select" all text on a particular page or in an active window.
- Command + B: To make "Bold" a text selected.
- Command + I: To "Italicize" a text selected.
- Command + U: To "Underline" a text selected.

Working with apps and files

Keyboard shortcuts can be used to switch, open and close applications. While working on a file, like Microsoft Word Doc, various shortcuts can be used in creating new files, finding words as well as printing.

- **Option + Command + Esc:** This shortcut key is used to force quit a program that is frozen or not responding. It forces to open a dialog box for force Quitting Apps. There you can now choose an app and tap "Force Quit" to quit it.

- **Command + Delete:** It sends a file selected file to Trash.

- **Enter:** It "Opens" a file or app selected.

- **Space:** To "Preview" a file selected.

- **Command + N:** To "Create" a new file.

- **Command + O:** To "Open" a file already existing.

- **Command + S:** To "Save" a present file.

- **Command + Z:** To "Undo" a preceding action. You can choose to "Redo" the action if you wish, tap "Command + Y" (or "Command + Shift + Z" in certain applications).

Internet shortcuts

Keyboard shortcuts can as well be used in navigating the web browser. A lot of the shortcuts for text above can as well be useful online, as well as the shortcuts for copying, pasting and selecting text into a web browser's address bar. Take note that few of these shortcuts can also work somehow differently; it all depends on the kind of browser you use.

- **Command + N**: To "Open" a new window browser.
- **Command + T**: To "Open" a new tab browser.
- **Command + D**: To "Bookmark" a current page.
- **Command + B**: To "View" your bookmarks.
- **Command + J**: To "View" files downloaded in recent times.

Locating more shortcuts on your keyboard

In a lot of apps, you'll locate keyboard shortcuts close to menu items. If you look for your shortcuts in this manner, you'll observe that macOS uses a few symbols that are different in indicating various keys on the keyboard, which includes:

- ⌘ - Command key
- ⇧ - Shift key
- ⌥ - Option key
- ^ - Control key
- fn - Function key
- While performing the shortcut ⌥ ⌘ P, tap "Option + Command + P" from your keyboard. ⇧ ⌘ S is "Shift + Command + S", etc.

CHAPTER FOURTEEN

COMMON APPLICATIONS FOUND IN MACOS

macOS has numerous apps that are useful and preloaded. Variety of tasks can be accomplished when you use just these applications without having to install others.

A lot of these applications can be opened by tapping their icon on your Dock beneath the screen. If you cannot find an application's icon on the Dock, you can find it by tapping the Launchpad icon.

Safari

It is a web browser used with easy and built up for Mac has a lot of similar features with other browsers. It's possible to bookmark and share among your devices, while a built-in menu enables you to share webpages through social media easily.

Mail

This app enables you to download your email to your PC and arrange it accordingly. Also acting as a new interface for your email with features such as Markup that enables you to draw on an attachment.

Calendar

The calendar helps in organizing your schedules using a color-coded interface. Views on a daily, weekly, monthly or yearly basis can easily be switched. It features some cooperating tools such as sharing, notifications and planning your trip.

Messages

Messages can be connected to different impromptu message services while organizing your chats all in a particular application. It supports audio and video chats as well including some other services.

iTunes

This application affords you the access to Apple's extensive online store of movies, TV shows and Music. It helps you to save and play your media from your computer and organizes your media into a custom playlist.

App Store

This app offers a unified way of searching for, purchasing and installing applications online. Also, help in automatic updates of your applications when you're doing other things.

Photos

Photo App helps to organize your photo, thereby giving you the permission of storing, sorting and displaying your photos from your computer. It also has features such as online storage, photo editor and ways you can share your photos online.

Time Machine

Time Machine helps you to automatically backup your files to a network server or an external hard drive. Immediately, it's configured, it performs an automatic backup regularly.

System Preferences

Adjusting the setting of your computer is done with "System Preferences." It comprises the configuration of different system settings, including options for personalizing some functions on your computer.

CONCLUSION

This book has revealed the step by step approach to macOS Big Sur for operation and maximum effectiveness.

The design has been refreshed by Apple considerably in its operating system and apps streamlining. Photos and mails look like iOS/iPadOS, while Notification Centre has a distinct view and this is happening for the very first time. Notifications now grouped concerning apps, and some of them are as well collaborating.

The Big Sur can easily be navigated and controlled by users. All you need has been developed on from the window curves corner to the amazing materials used and colors.

The Dock's icon is now designed more consistently with other icons in Apple's ecosystem.

The controls and Buttons are now appearing whenever they're needed and retreated whenever they aren't required.

A bar menu well customized, including a Control Center that is new and can bring fast control assessment from your desktop. For instance, from there, Wi-Fi and

Bluetooth controls are easily found including when playing music and enabling Dark Mode. Additionally, you can include your favorites.

GLOSSARY

Some IOS icons found in Big Sur

ABOUT THE AUTHOR

Eileen D. Rosenberg is a designer that specializes in system operation and hardware on Mac and PCs. she's passionate about the optimum satisfaction of users and how they gets updates frequently on security and upgrades.

She is a designer that enjoys digital photo editing, surfing the web, and listening to music.

Eileen D. Rosenberg was born in New Orleans, America. She specializes in using data and numbers to make an impactful design and has She has a deep understanding of software applications as well as issues relating to Mac and MacBook.

www.ingramcontent.com/pod-product-compliance
Lightning Source LLC
LaVergne TN
LVHW051657050326
832903LV00032B/3867